Victoria Bitter

Stories from an Australian Winter

by Alex Tannen

2nd Edition
January 2014
ISBN-13: 978-1492866480
ISBN-10: 1492866482

Contact, photos and information:
www.facebook.com/alex.tannen.ebook
alex.tannen.ebook@facebook.com

Cover: Mike Beuke, www.coolcad.de
Translated from the German by Katie Bedford
Photographs: Alex Tannen

From the Duniani series
All names have been changed
This book is also available as eBook

CONTENT

1   Introduction   5

2   The place – and the isolation   7

3   The people   9

4   The weather   11

5   Martin and the language   13

6   The beer   16

7   The food   21

8   The Royal Mail Hotel I: 23
    My Accommodation

9   The Royal Mail Hotel II: 25
    The Pub

10 Customs and Traditions   27

11 Work and Bureaucracy   29

12 48 hours with Bill I: 33
    The wild boar hunt

13 48 hours with Bill II: 42
    Behind enemy lines

14 Groovy Grapes   47

15   A Hot Ending   54

16   Worldvision Song Contest   57

     List of Transportation   66

     List of Superlatives   67

INTRODUCTION

1,300 inhabitants, 90 minutes to the next town – this isn't proper Outback for Australians. But it certainly is as far as the emotional life of a Berliner is concerned.

In 2003 I spent four months as a trainee in a construction company in a lonely little town called Lake Cargelligo, and I hardly left it during this time. Four months with affectionate, crude, one-of-a-kind builders, who call themselves *Bushies* and ingest enormous quantities of beer once the sun goes down. Alcohol is inevitably a recurring theme in these stories of my maverick colleagues and their day-to-day life on the geographical fringe of Australian society.

I landed in Australia in the winter... and was in for a surprise. It is a myth, sustained by shrewd marketing, that it is always warm Down Under. I only didn't freeze during those four months thanks to an improvised stove, built from a washing machine drum. By the end I was very glad that I hadn't done my traineeship in a swish ad agency in Sydney, but rather in the quiet backwater that was Lake Cargelligo.

Alex Tannen, October 2013

THE PLACE – AND THE ISOLATION

An off licence, two pubs, three petrol stations and four churches: my '*Praktikum*' or work experience, brought me to Lake Cargelligo, a town with 1,300 inhabitants on the edge of the Outback, 700 kilometers west of Sydney in the state of New South Wales. While the neighbouring land consists almost exclusively of bush and dry grassland, the town is set idyllically on the lake to which it owes its name.

The next town, Griffith, is 130 kilometres away, so Andie, my boss for the next few months was constantly picking me up in his Cessna 232. There weren't many alternatives to flying: there was a bus to a small town nearby, but only once a day.

Of course, many places in Australia are even more remote. But for these inhabitants, an hour and a half's drive to the dentist was clearly too much – every other set of teeth looked like it hadn't made the journey in many years. Otherwise, there were few reasons to leave the town – as the centre of the region Lake Cargelligo had a high street with a bakery, snack shops, a police station, half a dozen garages, a post office and a newsagent (latest editions available from 10am). The butcher stocked everything except kangaroo, and both supermarkets even offered sauerkraut. When I once bought the last four tins – it was my turn to cook and of course I served up the stereotype – new supplies were in one week later.

There, where it's not worth running a specialist shop, areas of business blend together. Mr Schneider, of German descent, who manned the pumps at the Shell garage, also acted as postman and repaired lawnmowers – which in Australia are almost as important as barbecues. The BP garage – also run by a German, Mr Heinz – housed the biggest video library of the town; the branch office of the state energy company Country Energy ran the internet cafe; and cars were registered in the library.

The town had everything one could want, right down to a hairdresser and the Salvation Army. And if someone needed a new DVD player or the latest Playstation game? Unlike the people with toothache, my new friend Bill would drive an hour and a half to Griffith for a newly released DVD alone. He would scarcely have the film in his hands before turning for home again. Bushies don't like towns.

THE PEOPLE

My colleagues primarily installed major water pipes, and were straight off the pages of a film script:

1. *George*: mid 40s, a Harley Davidson type with a grey Ho-Chi-Minh beard. He ended up in hospital when a 400kg pipe rolled into the trench where he was standing. It was my second day on the site. A miracle that he survived.

2. *Antony*: an intellectual ex-policeman, mid 50s. He was allegedly responsible for Georges's accident, and so voluntarily left the firm.

3. *Steve*: half Aboriginal, a replacement for George. An honest, reliable family man, he was the only one of the gang who came from Lake Cargelligo and didn't drink.

4. *Martin*: early 60s, an experienced bush pilot and ex-flying instructor with Opalmine, I couldn't understand a word he said. He was in charge purely of occupational safety and didn't himself get his hands dirty. He also flew the company's plane when something needed to be picked up from the hardware store. Aviation magazines and

a monthly paper with used diggers and bulldozers were his main reading material.

5. *Bill*: my best mate. A loveable hothead, 28 years old but looked 38. A rugby-player type with a 3-day beard, he drank 7 pints of Victoria Bitter beer a day, smoked 100 dollars worth of pot a week, played a lot of playstation martial-arts games, and hurtled through the bush on his 90 PS motorbike. The only thing missing in his life was a visit to Munich's Oktoberfest, which he raved about to me every day. He came from the town of Warren, as did Robert.

6. *Robert*: late 30s, a family man, who had already been caught drink driving 5 times and so had to work with us instead of being a lorry driver. When after countless mishaps, he finally filled a pipe trench with expensive sand instead of free waste soil, he was let go. Once previously, he had failed to properly secure a truck wheel after changing the tyre, and so while driving along the open road Andie was overtaken by the fourth wheel of his own truck.

7. *Andie*: the boss. Had emigrated from Germany with his parents 40 years ago as a 14 year old. I had to take care not to speak too much German with him. After all, I had come to Australia primarily to improve my English.

THE WEATHER

Since my arrival in Sydney at the beginning of June, coats and gloves were very much needed. Only I hadn't brought any to Australia. On tv they only show a permanently sun-drenched Bondi Beach. Or are those archive pictures? Of course I knew that there was a season called winter – I just thought it would be a bit cooler, not actually cold.

Inland, at Lake Cargelligo, the temperature sank to below zero at night. In the mornings, fields and windscreens were covered in frost, and the batteries in Andie's aeroplane were so flat that we needed a jumpstart to take off. The lake, a rarity in the Australian outback and therefore usually a centre for watersports, lay desolate for months. Although the sun beat down in the day, I would wear four or five layers of t-shirts, jumpers and jackets because the wind was bitter. The blue sky was only a pretence of summer – after dark it was icy again. Andie's potbellied stove was constantly lit in those months – actually an old washing machine drum, over which a cut-up, half barrel hung for smoke extraction.

Even during my travels after the time at Lake Cargelligo, the weather did not improve. In Adelaide it tipped it down the whole day, and my week in Western Australia was misty, dank, windy and rainswept. Only at photo stops did I have some luck: the sun came out for the most important moments – which must have been due to the people at Australian Weather Marketing.

My two single unadulterated summer weeks came in the north and in the heart of Australia, as well as in tropical Queensland. For the first time in months I wore shorts and mules.

Back in Sydney a week before my return flight, I once again had to pack away the lighter clothing. Although in Australia the seasons are the other way around, October suffers from typical autumnal weather there too – it rained on four out of my five days. To begin with I had a tv day; the next night I took an umbrella to the opera. Luckily, I already had lots of sunny pictures of Harbour Bridge from my first visit to Sydney, two years previously. Otherwise my friends at home would have realised that they do have clouds in Australia.

And then my departure for Europe. Australia wept bitterly.

MARTIN AND THE LANGUAGE

'Uh uh uheh?' gabbled the 60 year old man, who stood in a bomber jacket at Parkes station. His to me unintelligible, deep bass voice sounded like it was ringing out of a brass barrel.

Newly arrived, I had wanted to ring Andie in 300km-distant Lake Cargelligo to ask him to pick me up in his plane. But he had already sent someone for me.

The man introduced himself. 'Uh uhel', he said, which obviously meant that he was Martin. In addition to his pilot's jacket, he wore a cowboy hat, blue work trousers, and workman's boots.

'Uh uh uheh?', he asked me again. I thought for a moment. He wasn't speaking an Aboriginal language, he must have asked me, in English, 'Are you Alex?'

'Yes I'm Alex,' I responded after a short pause. Martin rang for a taxi, while I was relieved that being collected had worked out so quickly. The cab drove us to the airfield – and a short test revealed I had no problems understanding the taxi driver.

Martin readied the Cessna for take-off, constantly calling out to me, of which I deciphered barely a word. He didn't so much speak as roar, which meant that the words got compressed and 'Let's fly' sounded like 'uh uh'. It was difficult even after repeated enquiries to filter a single word from the general thundering.

My comprehension was also not improved when the aeroplane started and the noise of the motors filled the cabin. We entertained ourselves with the noisy voice radio: I yelled into the microphone, and he bellowed back. It's a mystery to me how the air traffic controller in Melbourne centre, more than 1,200 kilometres away, could give him his clearance for take-off.

We flew over dry bushland. A railway split the landscape, and a river meandered along next to it. So that we didn't sit side-by-side in complete silence, I tapped along the row of instruments in the cockpit, and he explained each one to me. Of course I understood not a word, but it passed the hour-long journey comfortably. 'We may as well turn round,' I thought to myself. 'If everyone here speaks like this, my English is not going to make much progress.'

Luckily, things turned out differently. Andie was German by birth, and Bill, Robert and Steve spoke halfway comprehensibly. They did speak quickly, but would immediately shift down a gear if they saw question marks in my eyes. Long evenings round the fire trained me well in S*trine*, the Australian accent. Of course they don't consider it an accent; they don't recognise British English as any benchmark. Purely in language terms, my learning encompassed million-dollar pipeline deals, Terminator films (in which naturally little was said), and the customary topics: women, hunting wild boar, drought, corrupt politicians, and unique, true, country life.

In fact those were also Martin's topics. In the evenings he liked to tell jokes, which are perhaps the hardest and most demanding part of a language. 'Martin, can you please speak more clearly?' I would ask.

'No, I cannot', he would answer, mercilessly.

I had communication problems right up till the end. After three months he said to me 'Uh uh uh uh uh uh.'

I shook my head. 'Sorry?'

'Uh uh uh uh uh uh', the coded message was again transmitted.

I thought it over. What? Oh! 'POST – GO – NOW!' I climbed into the car and went to post the letters.

I consoled myself with the fact that even Bill sometimes had difficulty in deciphering his secret code. We both therefore named Martin 'Goldberg' – after the character in Police Academy whose shrill voice was equally unintelligible. Andie had no such troubles. He had known Martin for more than 30 years and had learnt to fly from him. He had obviously understood what the instruments in the cockpit meant – even at the beginning, he had never had an accident.

THE BEER

None of the customers could articulate normally anymore. Women danced on tables. Teenagers raced about in high spirits. Most punters stood drinking together in small circles and shouted at each other; and because everyone did that, everyone shouted louder. In the gents' toilets, three drunk blokes were peeing in the direction of the wall from 2 yards away – obviously a competition as to who could reach the furthest.

Every Saturday night, the young people in Lake Cargelligo met at the Bowling Club with one aim: to get plastered. There was no real conversation, no pleasant sitting together, and no appreciation of a drink – in the glaringly-lit hall the goal was as simple as on Männertag[1] in Germany, only here it was at least once a week and was celebrated by everyone. Regardless of gender or skin colour, everyone got drunk in record time. Even Jimmy, the Royal Mail Hotel landlord joined in. He closed his premis-

---

1 Nominally Fathers' Day in Germany, when traditionally men would do a hiking tour with beer and food, but now largely an excuse for getting absolutely wasted.

es and drove the guests in a booze bus to his rival. The middy glasses (half pint) were only half empty before he ordered refills. It was no surprise that so much change lay on the floor at the counter that I could buy myself two small glasses – of light beer, of course.

Not due to alcohol, but due to good old fashioned Australian hospitality, came an invitation from Peter, an employee away on business, to stay with him in Sydney before I flew back to Germany. He had spoken to me at the bar, because I had pronounced 'beer' too like 'Bier', and he liked Germany. I raved to him about how I would love to live in Sydney. 'No problem', said Peter, who was still at that stage half sober. He wouldn't be there, but I could spend a few days at his flat alone. I could pick up the key from his father and simply slam the door when I was done. I just mustn't touch the new flat screen tv. And that's how it happened. Except for that half hour in the pub, we wouldn't see each other again before he handed over a smart apartment in central Sydney.

The skinny checkout girl from the supermarket, who was drinking next to us, also had a certain affinity with Germany. 'Heil Hitler! Schnell, schnell!', she raised her glass to me. Those were the only words she could remember from her German father.

Nine or ten pints of beer a night wasn't unusual. I was proudly told that Australia drank more than Germany during Oktoberfest. Newspapers printed the sober truth: 39 percent of all Australians consume alcohol in quantities that can cause long-term health problems, not including those who are too young to purchase alcohol and who don't appear in the statistics. Most of those stay home and smoke pot. Some Aborigines in the club were only sober because they had already lost their welfare money on the three fruit machines. Wages and unemployment benefit were paid weekly for that reason. Otherwise many Australians would spend half the month broke – and probably drying out.

However, I was the only one who showed myself up: because the booze hall was actually a bowling club, and it is against the rules to wear a hat in an Australian club, everyone cried out in horror when I came in with a pirate-style cloth on my head. A lot of value is placed on correct behaviour. But they didn't throw me out or threaten to ban me – following tradition the crowd simply demanded I buy a round. Happily I was able to excuse myself as a foreigner, albeit without returning their 'Heil Hitler' greeting...

In the weeks that followed, the alcohol excesses in the Royal Mail Hotel, one of the two pubs, went further. The rugby club 'The Tigers' had won a regional championship. Every player was drunk for three days, not a single teammate could withstand the group pressure. It was too much even for Jimmy. He unceremoniously pressed the pub keys into the hands of the men, and took himself off to bed.

A further opportunity for cheap drinking was offered every Wednesday in the pub promotion 'Toss the Boss'. The toss of a coin decided whether a customer had to pay for his beer or not. There was nothing to lose. 'Tails' in fact meant the kangaroo tail on the back of a former Australian coin, but practical as always, no coins were actually thrown, but a dice with three 'T's and three 'H's. It was quicker that way. Family man Robert's monthly balance, with 10 out of 12 beers free, was clearly a statistical impossibility. He claimed the game had only lasted an hour and he'd had no more than three beers...

Most customers were so drunk that it was obvious to me why each round had to be paid for immediately. It saved lengthy discussions at the end of the night, and every drinker knew throughout the evening how much money they still had. Although I wouldn't call it tight budgeting: the change simply lay on the bar. As soon as the schooner or bottle was approaching the bottom, the barmaid brought refills, and took the money from the pile. Should the pile at some point run out, no one need go thirsty. Running a tab was illegal, and with no barman wanting to give credit to the alcohol-addled, short-term memoried, the solution was amazingly simple: a cash machine in the pub. A customer had to only remember his pin in order to stay solvent.

Beer was often hard currency. If Andie dug out a neighbour's driveway with his digger, or heaved a farmer's car out of the ditch, he would be asked 'what's your poison?', and 20 minutes later a carton of Hahn Light stood as a thank you on the table, which he mostly didn't touch. In the same way, Andie could appease the young men from the utility companies when he had destroyed another of their pipes.

Australians always stay true to their beer. Andie drank exclusively Hahn Light, Martin swore by Hahn Premium, and Robert and Bill would knock back only Victoria Bitter – known as VB – which, they said, was the only good thing to come out of the neighbouring state of Victoria. They defended their choices as vehemently as a favourite rugby team. Only there's one thing that's even more important: the correct refrigeration. Or more accurately, deep cooling. In the pub, customers could specify the appropriate temperature for their beer; at home they had to take care of it themselves. Because a bottle which had not been inside a fridge for several hours is gnat's piss. For this reason, many people had fridges with only beer inside. The first thing the men in our builders' camp thought of in the morning was beer. Not because their dry stomachs needed a drink, but because far-sightedly and almost lovingly, they put their six pack in the fridge. Then when work finished, their first movement was to reach for a bottle. Screw top, so you didn't even have to find an opener. After the first long swig, helmets were put down and work was signed off for the day. After that they drank without a break, until they fell into bed. By day, at work, they didn't touch a drop – probably the only reason that they were still alive.

So that pub customers didn't have to drive themselves, pubs were obliged to provide a courtesy bus after 10pm to drive people home. Jimmy also happily picked people up. Despite this, Robert and Bill had already been caught drink driving 5 times. Surely you can only be that stupid when you have alcohol in the blood. If they should be caught a sixth time, they would go to prison – a judge had already passed a precautionary six-month sentence, they told me with a mixture of fear and pride.

The amount consumed in pubs was fuelled by the method of reciprocal rounds. No one paid only for himself, but always for his companions as well. As soon as the first glass was empty, new drinks were ordered, even if his friends were nowhere near finished. As the fresh beer was drawn, the old drinks were quickly downed. And those who had already paid took care that the others quickly repaid their debt by heading to the bar – 'It's your shout, mate!' At the end of the evening, the drinks would keep coming until everyone was quits. And then, just as they were almost out of the door, it would occur to someone that they could still have 'one for the road'. And of course the new round lasted until everyone had taken his turn, 'four for the road'.

This system of payment worked particularly well because in the pubs of New South Wales there were no large glasses. Jimmy told me that the half-litre sized 'pints' were abolished so that people weren't tempted into getting drunk. What rubbish. Just like the huge, state-prescribed notices which hung in pubs and were supposed to prevent excessive alcohol consumption. The central message of these notices was 'We don't serve drunks'.

THE FOOD

Thanks to Andie, meals were excellent. He was a keen amateur cook and every night served good home cooking: stuffed peppers, oxtail soup or potato bake. Although everyone praised his culinary skill in the highest terms, the workers doused the roulade in ketchup. Lentil soup can apparently be eaten with a fork – although I didn't master the backhand cutlery manoeuvre until the end of my stay. If any soup was left over, they would smear it onto bread the next morning and stick it in the microwave for one minute.

A whole other gastronomical world awaited in Griffith, an hour and a half away, where Andie, Martin and I once made a trip. It's a town of 30,000 inhabitants, dominated by Italians. A vast, undulating wine-growing region ensured the appropriate mediterranean mood and excellent wine. In dozens of pizzerias, restaurants and street cafes the raw Outback could be forgotten for a few hours amongst carpaccios and cafe lattes.

Back in Lake Cargelligo – whose name at least sounded Italian – I experienced the culinary lowpoint of the week: a completely carbonised piece of toast, which I had earlier tossed in the bin, was deemed 'totally edible' by everybody, and eaten up without hesitation. We stared at each other, equally stunned.

Despite the significant influence of Italian immigrants – bodies were allegedly once pulled out of the river by Griffith with their feet embedded in concrete – Australia is apparently the only country in the world where you need a knife to eat spaghetti. But my culinary habits were strange to Australian palates. Six weeks after I added vinegar to my lentil soup I was still being reproached for this 'disgusting' transgression. I provoked a heated debate when I took Worcester sauce from the shelf to add to my pork chop. Although my colleagues swamped every meal in strange sauces, it seemed I had gone too far: Worcester sauce belonged with t-bone steak, naturally, but absolutely not with pork chops – that was what apple sauce was for.

THE ROYAL MAIL HOTEL I:
MY ACCOMODATION

Since 1898 the Royal Mail Hotel had provided beer and cheap rooms, and as far as furnishing and comfort was concerned, it seemed not much had changed in the last century. The frame of my bed was utterly knackered and the mattress sagged virtually to the floor. I sank down, found no hold, and swam my way through the night. The next morning my limbs hurt and I struggled to stand up. I asked for a new room.

The next night I threw myself exhausted onto my new berth – and fell through again: it too was as soft as butter. But was I not working for a building firm? Since I didn't want to go through all the beds in the hotel, I sawed myself a wide board at work, and placed it under the mattress.

The door to my windowless room led to a saloon style terrace. Unfortunately, the door had a huge crack. In summer, a practical ventilation tool, but not when the temperature dropped to below zero at night. It was freezing, but neither the electric blanket nor the bar heater on the wall worked. I decided to warm myself up with a hot shower, and shivered my way across the back courtyard. But the electric was off there too, and the lamps remained black. But for 50 dollars a week I didn't want to complain. The neighbouring motel cost 70 dollars for one night. I showered by torchlight, and resolved to bring a fan heater from work.

During the 11 weeks I was there, the maid didn't change my hand towel once. Luckily, I found the store room and helped myself. The only way I knew of the hotel staff's existence was that every day the blankets were tucked tight under the mattress. Literally welded under there. I practically dislocated my shoulder pulling them out. That the bedding was changed as frequently as the hand towels didn't matter – the cold forced me to sleep in my own sleeping bag.

At night Jimmy locked the main entrance. To get into the hotel I had to go through the back courtyard which was guarded by his Blue Heeler – a merciless breed of dog, as I later discovered. Treating me as a burglar, he ran at me with teeth bared. Initially I was protected by the short chain which held him to the kennel, but later Jimmy tethered him with a wire rope which could run the length of the yard. He was still tolerable, because with time he seemed to get used to me. More aggressive was his companion, a yappy little lapdog, who would wake the Blue Heeler (who would mostly otherwise sleep through my arrival). This ball of wool would bite furiously at my heels, or jump up at me, as if challenging his friend to finally snap. The Blue Heeler however lay lazily on his back and let himself be stroked. There was nothing in the hotel worth stealing anyway.

On the penultimate day of my stay, the bulb went in my dim ceiling light. It apparently being too difficult to change a lightbulb, Jimmy moved me to a different room. He obviously wanted to do something nice for me just as I was leaving. In this spotless bed in the unexpectedly large and bright room next door, I could have spent a much more pleasant couple of months.

THE ROYAL MAIL HOTEL II: THE PUB

Customers queued to warm themselves by the fire. Frost had got into their limbs, and they bobbed shivering from foot to foot. Half of Lake Cargelligo was defrosting themselves in the Royal Mail Hotel, and the blazing fire made the pub a cosy snug. Some people seemed to have moved in and were half attached to the bar. Long-divorced couples were again sharing a table.

The pub was kitted out with everything an Australian pub should have: several television screens mounted on the ceiling, a fruit machine area, a darts corner, a map of Australia on the wall, and yellowing pictures of local rugby team *The Tigers*. Only the opening times and the attendance of patrons was a mystery to me. Some Fridays, no surprise, the pub was full to bursting, but then a week later no more than ten people would be whiling away time at the bar. A full Friday did not guarantee a good Saturday – Saturday seemed to be the day that least went on, so that Jimmy, the bar owner, closed the earliest, mostly around 10pm. Still he always gave us five minutes to drink up before throwing us out. Then unexpectedly in the middle of the week, things would keep going till midnight. Never longer, because that was closing time. Although I was rarely in the Guest Saloon, I knew exactly what went on there because my bedroom was over the pub.

The most important thing in the pub, without which business wouldn't have been half so good, was the service, that is, the barmaids. At the end of the day, it mattered to Andie, Robert and Martin (the pub was too expensive for Bill) who served them. Every evening they wondered aloud in their camp: who is working tonight? Jimmy had only women working for him, because it noticeably improved profits when a regular could watch how a girl bent over to get another bottle from the fridge. To better distinguish between them, we gave each of them nicknames:

1. *The Dyke* was so called because she made the others think of a stand-offish lesbian, with her angular face and short hair. She had a child. As her main job she worked in the supermarket.

2. *The German* wanted to know on my first evening how to say 'How are you going?' in German. Since then, she greeted me with a friendly and accent-free 'Wie geht es dir?' and said 'Danke'. When she asked me to translate 'Goodbye' at closing time, I knew it was time to take my leave. She was the nicest of them all – in fact the only nice one.

3. *The Model* was thin, pretty, and of course arrogant. We never learned anything more about her, because she did only the bare minimum and was not in any way talkative.

4. *Heidi* was Heidi. Previously known as Heinz, she was the daughter of a BP petrol pump attendant of German origin. She was married with two children, but nevertheless Andie – who was twice as old as she was – believed he could end up with her. She was the chief reason that he came to the pub. Jimmy thought the same.

CUSTOMS AND TRADITIONS

1. If two men go to the cinema together, they must under no circumstances sit next to each other. Otherwise they are obviously gay.
2. At the meat counter at the supermarket, you take a number and wait until you are called.
3. Driving on the left goes for supermarket aisles as well.
4. There are no one or two cent coins. If the price comes to an odd number it is rounded up or down. Bill would always try to put two cents more petrol in his car than he had to pay for.
5. Australian banknotes are made of very thin plastic. You can wash them.
6. Every fortnight is Pension Weekend when benefits are paid. Pubs are full, and there is more fighting and vandalism in the streets. For this reason you learn to park your car round the back.
7. Typically Australian products – peanut butter for example – have emblazoned on them that they were produced in Australia and that the company is run by Australians. With such patriotic purchases, one could ensure native jobs, taxes, and the future of the entire con-

tinent. There was an advert for an Australian pizza chain outside the headquarters of American *Pizza Hut* which read reprovingly 'Surely you don't want our profits going here?'

WORK AND BUREAUCRACY

You think Germany is bureaucratic? As far as regulation is concerned, Australia seems to consider everything much more thoroughly than we do. There is no longer any trace of the lawless Bush romanticism, where everyone can do what he likes. Australian businesses complain that a worker's every move requires a special certificate. On the fifth continent, 'ticket' has become the most important word on a building site.

Andie's four-man construction company laid a water pipeline at the edge of the Outback. It ran from the lake to a water reservoir tower and then on to house connections. If he dug up a road to lay a pipe, or narrowed a crossroads for a couple of hours, traffic could only go in one direction – if there was traffic. Even if only two cars an hour passed the dust track, we all had to attend an official Traffic Control Seminar, in essence to learn how to correctly hold a Stop-and-Slow sign.

The police-like regulating authority, WorkCover, had clearly strengthened this and other industrial safety rules. Drastic punishments which could quickly ruin a firm would help 'achieve the safest workplaces in the world'. Because previously, building sites were pretty much as relaxed as Bondi Beach. Result: too many industrial accidents. That must change. Equally responsible for the current wave of regulations – about which employers and employees groaned equally – was the often all too lacking training. Newcomers, unskilled labourers and temps were often on site. Knowledge which in Germany would be learned during training, in Australia had to be acquired through extra courses. Another reason for the avalanche of rules, according to Andie, was growth of the US custom of suing following an accident. It was thought that through the prescribed training courses, licences, and tickets, you could guard against such things.

The well-meant security craze had strange effects. As one of only four employees in Andie's company, Martin was occupied exclusively by industrial safety and the firm's compliance with regulations. He was the obligatory Safety Officer. The most important of his tasks was to constantly check whether everyone was wearing orange signal vests and helmets. That extended to employees – out in the open and far from any machinery – taking a crate out of a car. A WorkCover inspector might appear at any moment, and fear of officials ran deep. Martin's favourite pastime – also governmentally enforced – was to organise a meeting point at which the four workers should gather after an accident. This place was marked by an iron stake in the ground with a skittle on top of it. When the pipeline advanced a few hundred metres in a day, the gathering point came too. Of course the point had to be far enough away from the potential accident site. If left and right of the pipeline stretched boggy pasture, then in boggy pasture must be the gathering point, even when the fleeing workers would have to machete their way through the tall grass to reach the point of salvation. Apparently more construction workers had died from snake bites at gathering points than through accidents.

To drive a construction vehicle, you needed an extra ticket – the normal lorry drivers' licence wouldn't do. If you were allowed to drive trucks, that did not allow you to drive bulldozers. Robert had to carry each individual licence on him, so his wallet was as thick as if he had every available credit card. Training must be regularly repeated, to the delight of the providers of these appropriate, fee-based courses. Sometimes the seminars took place in a faceless office in the next town, sometimes in Andie's camp by the fire.

Electricians could also rub their hands with glee, since thanks to the law they could barely keep up with demand for their work. All electrical devices on a company's premises had to be checked every single month. This doesn't affect just drills and circular saws, but also in Andie's case every piece of equipment in the workers' lodgings. So the four fridges were inspected, the tv, the toaster, the microwave, and the well-used, of course electric, grill. In total the electrician looked at 17 household items – quickly checking whether the cable was intact. A compliance sticker alone, which must adorn every plug, cost one dollar. The electrician got 100 dollars (70 euros) for his work. Nice work if you can get it.

Martin Prellberg, lecturer and examiner in occupational safety, was a very busy man. He ran the infamous Occupational Health and Safety Training. No one, not a truck driver, self-employed painter or checkout girl in the diy store could do a stroke of work without passing his course. Prellberg also ran our one-day Traffic Control Seminar, prescribed by the Roads and Traffic Authority (RTA) of New South Wales. As state-inaugurated teacher, he first gave an overview of the important tools: the Stop and Slow sign, the dazzling, reflective protective vest, and a walkie-talkie with which to communicate with colleagues. Compulsory, due to the supposed Australian climate, were hat, sunglasses, longsleeved top, long trousers, stout shoes and sun cream with a factor of at least 30. Everyone must have the logos of their employer and the RTA emblazoned on their top. Films and graphics exemplified for us the rights, regulations, hand signs and correct procedure for how we should stop a car on a road narrowed to one lane, and after a short time let it continue.

We spent almost half a day of the seminar on bureaucracy. The paperwork was as elaborate as if we were applying for citizenship. First we filled in the form which asked whether we spoke a language other than English at home. 'Arabic, Cantonese, Hindi or Tagalog?' German was considered to have died out and was not an option. Then we completed a list of participants, keeping our names and signatures separate. Eventually the examiner gave out the application form for the RTA licence. Then we had to mark an A4 sheet with our registration number and sign it in large letters, and, as if we were being listed on the sex offenders register, had to hold the paper in front of ourselves and be photographed for identification. After that, a simple application form from the semi-governmental operators of the course in order to participate, before we had to fill out a statement for the conclusion of the seminar. Later we received our Traffic Control Logbook, which we must in future keep on us and in which we must document all operations. Everyone must enter his name and official registration number. At the end of it all, the lecturer requested a written appraisal of his work.

Whether we learnt anything was completely by-the-by. The test consisted of a dozen easy multiple choice questions. Copying from a neighbour and prompting by the teacher included.

48 HOURS WITH BILL I:
THE WILD BOAR HUNT

A red-glowing sandstorm darkened the view north like a curtain. From the south, a black wall of rain edged its way forward. We hurried to leave the town.

Faced with this treacherous weather, Andie had brought the weekend forward and given us Thursday and Friday off. I took Bill up on his offer of joining him on a trip to his home town of Warren. It was almost 400km away, or – since it's traditional to measure distances in beer – some five to seven bottles. 'Drink and drive' in Australia doesn't mean getting sozzled at a party or in the pub and then driving, but rather combining the two. 'No worries Alex! I drive the safest when I've had a couple,' said Bill, reassuringly. 'Yeah, and smoked some pot,' I added.

Before we set off for four hours through the Bush, we had to visit not only the petrol station and cash machine, but also the off licence and pot dealer. An hour and a half later than planned we set off. The sandstorm we had wanted to flee was already close behind us.

When I began my placement at Andie's outback firm, Bill adopted me. Since then he had guided me in all matters of Bush life. He was a solidly built, salt-of-the-earth

type, proud of his Scottish-Irish roots as well as his true
Bushie nature. He hated towns and townspeople, and was
only happy out in the countryside. Bill used to be a rugby
player and allegedly earned his living from it. Today his
beer belly would hinder him from running an opponent
down. I found it hard to see him as 28 years old, as his
plump face made him look 10 years older. On his neck,
chest hair mingled with his 10-day beard. A battered cowboy hat covered his sparse hair, which sprang out in the
places it still grew. He turned up the collar of his fleece
jacket. Like almost all Outback inhabitants, he was unso-
phisticated, a bit raw, but extremely hospitable and kind –
as long as a cool beer was somewhere nearby. His greatest
wish was to visit Munich's Oktoberfest. He normally returned to this topic once a day, calling it 'Beer Festival'.
After all, it wasn't the rollercoasters he was interested in. If
he only had a week free to make the obligatory overseas
trip, he would head for Munich and spend the happiest
days of his life. He was therefore particularly grateful for
my tip that Oktoberfest actually takes place in September.

We drove east, in the direction of Condobolin, and it
looked as though the sandstorm would hit the rain directly
on this road. So that Bill could open his first beer, I held
the steering wheel. At that exact moment, an echidna – a
hedgehog-like creature – made its way onto the road. An
instinctive swing of my right hand prevented us ending our
journey in prickles after 10 minutes.

After Bill opened his second bottle we swapped places,
so that he finally had his other hand free to hold a joint.

Everywhere in the Bush seems to be arranged distance-
wise so as to allow bottles to be refilled. Of course, you
could stash a whole crate in the car, but Bill had no
coolbox and so was dependent on regular cold refills. Woe
betide anyone selling beer warmer than just above freezing.
That would be as unpleasant as alcohol-free liquid. In
Condobolin, 120km later, he ordered two more almost
frozen beers, which were each wrapped in a paper bag,

apparently the better to hold their temperature. (Unless otherwise stated, all alcohol is in 1.5 pint bottles, also called king browns, long necks, largies or tallies.)

The rain became heavier, and it poured down like the tropics. The rain had somehow swallowed the sandstorm. It was pitch dark and bleak. In Condobolin we had to decide whether to take the shorter route over a sand track, or the safer tarmac road, which would take an hour longer. At the petrol station they recommended we took the direct route over the track since storms hadn't been reported from that direction. We believed them, and ten minutes later the windscreen wiper was running at top speed. We now had to battle through a hundred kilometres of lonely sand road as far as Tottenham. It was unlikely we would meet another car, especially in this weather. If we got stuck, we still had Bill's motorbike which was in the back of the truck. He could get help with that, hopefully from Alcoholics Anonymous.

It was already an hour since we last saw a car, and the wall of rain sucked all the light from the headlights. Water shot up like lightning from the deep puddles. On either side of us lay Bush, from which at any moment a kangaroo could spring in front of the car – and Bill's car was of course the only one without a kangaroo catcher on the bonnet. Anyway, the heavy Nissan pick-up truck (which in Australia isn't called a pick up, but rather a 'ute') handled as clumsily as a lorry. Since I had no desire to smash a kangaroo, and since my slow pace of driving played havoc with Bill's distance-dependent drinking tempo, he took over once again. Not a kilometre too soon. His eyes were still just about open enough to see the kangaroo in time, as it sprang through the light from our headlamps. Masterfully he braked and swerved, and the beer bottle between his legs didn't spill a drop.

In Bill's glove compartment was a single CD. Instead of listening from beginning to end, he switched more than 20 times between his favourite three songs. At the beginning of each, he booted up the volume, and I automatically turned it down. Meanwhile he drove round bends as if he was on the track at Dakar. Bumps and pot holes shook us about, while the rain made the ground so slippery that we slid more than the tires gripped. 'Hopefully we'll reach tarmac before the road completely disappears into slush,' I thought.

Eventually we reached Tottenham, and since Bill had already emptied four long necks on the journey, he hid from an oncoming police car in a side street. We quickly changed places, because he'd already been caught drink driving five times. After his last accident (a complete write-off), the judge had put him on probation. Next time, he'd be looking at six months in prison, so he told me. Bill therefore basically didn't drive after his second beer – at least not unless it was a tricky, remote, cross-country road and he had a city boy next to him.

Naively, I thought that once in the pub at Tottenham he would finally phone his mother to let her know we were coming (he had no mobile). Instead of which, he picked up two new King Browns, and was straight back on the road. Bill impressed on me that when avoiding an oncoming vehicle or when slowing down, I must not under any circumstances have all four wheels off the road and on the verge. 'With this weather we would slip completely into the Bush. So move over first with two wheels, brake, and then stop completely on the left,' he told me, expertly.

Shortly before Nevertire I saw neatly illustrated what happens if you don't obey these rules. In front of us a Toyota stood diagonally across the road. We couldn't tell which direction it had originally come from. I executed a perfect stop just as Bill had instructed me. Soaked through, and wearing only a t-shirt, a young driver with a desperate expression peered through the window. His fuming girl-friend sat in the car. 'There have been no cars for an hour,' he said, 'Can you pull me out?' Although he'd already had five too many, Bill couldn't let someone else pull a car out of the mud. Afterwards I was allowed back at the wheel.

Nevertire was a pitstop 30 kilometres from our destination. In the days of the conquest of this continent, it lay at the halfway point on the four-day journey between two towns, and it was not advisable to get tired here or settle down for a nap. Bill told me, legend had it that the town got its name from a fearless Aborigine who would not surrender to the Britons. He apparently fought on alone against the colonial masters and settlers, and killed anyone who stepped on his territory.

Nevertire was completely destroyed 100 years ago by a hurricane. Today, only 170 people live there, too small for a pub or bottle shop. We drove on through, and just before Bill expired from thirst we reached his hometown of Warren. Warren had 2,000 inhabitants, a small high street, a supermarket, two pubs, and – much more importantly – a drive-through off licence. Before we collapsed at his parents', Bill was keen to first test the beer temperature there.

After successful replenishment – as we know, Bill drank exclusively Victoria Bitter – he let me wind through the empty main streets and in the absence of better attractions, take the roundabout twice. Then we drove to a friend, who Bill had been talking up extensively over the last 10 days for two reasons: he had German roots, and was his best friend. His name was Danny Randolph Fritsch, and was known as Dr because of his initials. Of course nobody could pronounce Fritsch properly. Here it was 'fridge', which gave the family the nickname 'Snow'.

Doctor Frost opened the door to us and Bill made clear we were as good as blood brothers. I was booked straightaway to meet Dr's German father the following day. After both had smoked a joint, and Dr's girlfriend had explained that it wasn't a sand storm, but rather a dust storm, we made our way to Bill's parents. And since there was only one beer left, we went again via the two lane drive-through highway.

In front of his parents' house, Bill drummed into me

that I shouldn't under any circumstances go alone towards the garden. A bull terrier was on guard there, and he didn't yet know me. Afterwards, he introduced me – to the dog. Ever practical as the Australians are, the dog was called Axle. After a little sniffing, I was accepted, which wasn't necessarily mutual. Then we rang the bell and got the parents out of bed. Bill's mum answered the door in her dressing gown, surprised by this visit from her son. Somehow he had forgotten to let her know we were coming. Bill greeted them quickly and then disappeared immediately into his room, embarrassed by his alcoholic odour and ten-day beard. I stayed alone with his mother, making conversation in front of the fire, while Bill showered, shaved, and got ready. As soon as he was done, Bill bolted for the front door calling 'Good night!' to his mother – and we were gone. 'Where are we going?' I asked.

'To some friends. We can go wild boar hunting with them for a few days.'

Everyone I met during my time in the Australian Bush wanted me to go wild boar hunting with them. However, since a shooting in a Tasmanian school ten years previously, private ownership of weapons was strictly forbidden – although hardly anyone had given up their rifle – and so the rural population could only hunt with dogs. The dogs chase the boars, and bite down onto them once caught. If the hunter gets to the unfortunate animal in time, he can perhaps still do something for it – or perhaps do something for his dogs, since a boar's tusks often mean things turn out differently than expected. Like zoo trips in other places, wild boar hunting was there an established family leisure activity. Children are taken from a young age, so that they learn early that there is nothing strange about a boar being torn to shreds. Like locusts, the animals are seen as nothing but a pest.

Bill's friend Harry opened the door to us a little absently. His girlfriend lay hunched in a chair and didn't even manage a nod in greeting. Beer bottles lay spread on the floor, with dirty plates nearby. Harry turned away and applied himself hastily to another drag on his joint. Their three-year-old child entertained himself with a cartoon film. It was just after 11pm.

As if it were illegal, Bill produced his beer from inside his coat. I was forced to stay dry – evidently it would ruin a host in Australia to offer his guests a drink.

When Bill introduced me, it always went like this: 'This is Alex from Germany. I'm his English teacher.' The reaction was normally a disbelieving grin, at which point Bill would rattle out a list of words he had taught me, which only widened people's smiles. With these introductions out of the way, he would come to the point: 'Alex would like to go on a boar hunt.' I would protest, but my pal simply couldn't understand how I could have anything against this pastime. According to popular belief, the creatures were all exported to France and Germany because we quite obviously ate wild boar every day.

Somehow I always managed to excuse myself, including this time. 'What a shame,' said Harry, 'But we can show you a video of the hunt.

'Jonny!' he shouted to the child, 'do you want to show your uncle the wild boar film?' And as if he were swapping Mickey Mouse for Miss Piggy, the child stopped his cartoon, took the film down from the shelf and put it in the machine.

'Daddy!' exclaimed the boy and tapped with his finger on the screen: two off-road vehicles were patrolling through the Bush. The grass was high. Everyone was tense, manically sweeping the area for boar. Swinging and zooming, the cameraman searched too. 'There!' screamed someone suddenly. The cars sped forward. Then they let the dogs out – a bull terrier, a rottweiler and a bull mastiff. They had been given blood to lick, and now raced barking out of the truck bed. With the camera running in his hand, Harry came a minute behind them. I felt dizzy. And the pig squealed for its life.

When the camera reached the slaughter scene, the carnage was in full flow. The three dogs had locked themselves on the boar's head and neck, and the animal defended itself only weakly, blood streaming over its hide. Everyone stared enraptured at the tv. The boy watched as if Tom was clobbering Jerry. They commentated on each scene as if it was a rugby game. The men in the film had trouble pulling the dogs off the dead pig. In their killing frenzy, the dogs had chewed down and the hide couldn't yield any more. At that moment the woman in the chair spoke for the first time, probably having been woken by the familiar programme. 'Bill, I'm not sure your friend likes it,' she ventured. There was no sympathy in her voice, but rather bewilderment, as if we were in Rio and I didn't want to go to Carnival. Bill babbled something, and his glazed eyes stared as loyally as the dogs' pre being let off the chain.

Before we left, the child put on a film of their holiday in Queensland. Highlight: the bloodthirsty komodo dragons in Brisbane Zoo.

Back at Bill's house he asked me mysteriously into his room. He closed the door and laid his finger on his lips, his expression serious. 'What I'm about to show you is strictly forbidden,' he whispered conspiratorially. Then he crawled under his bed and pulled out a bundle of blankets. He carefully unrolled the layers. 'It's a family heirloom, made in England, over 100 years old.' With quick movements he put the pieces together and proudly handed me the whole – a shotgun. It was double barrelled, very heavy. On the shaft I could make out elaborate carvings. I turned the gun over in the light and nodded appreciatively. We were still whispering. Bill took the weapon back, aimed and made as if to shoot. He stood opposite me swaying and breathing deeply. It seemed as if he was balancing the rifle. Eventually he dismantled the weapon, wrapped it carefully, and stowed it back in its hiding place. 'My granddad gave it to me to hold for the family. I'll never part with it,' he whispered. Then he unlocked his bedroom door again.

Before I headed off to bed, I had to send Bill to the medicine cabinet. Although I hadn't drunk a drop, I urgently needed a strong headache tablet.

48 HOURS WITH BILL II:
BEHIND ENEMY LINES

I was woken by Metallica. Shortly after 10am Bill turned his stereo up full volume. And to be completely sure that I was awake, he hammered on my door. 'It's late, we must get going', he shouted, and threw out a few suggestions for the day: 'A Bush trip, motorbike ride, maybe someone's doing a boar hunt somewhere'. He hadn't scheduled any breakfast. Not from lack of hospitality, it simply didn't belong to his morning routine. Instead he offered me a Hahn Premium Beer, his being already nearly empty. I managed to get a Nescafe and some toast, while Bill honked the horn outside. The off licence was calling.

After that he felt better, and since there was no boar hunt fun to be had, we wound our way through the town with Axle and the motorbike on the truck. Every few metres we had to stop to greet acquaintances of Bill. Punctually at the second bottle he let me take over the wheel.

After a short, half-hour trip into the Bush – filled with crazy stories of the type 'here is where my friend had a shoot-out with the police' – we called on Brad, one of

Bill's Aboriginal friends, who had his terraced house near-by.

The six pack was swiftly dispatched. I refused a second beer, 'Thanks, but I'm still driving'. Even if it was only to the off licence. Bill found the bottles too measly, and arriving in the bottle shop, finally grasped the relationship between the small bottle volume and the frequency with which he had to refill. We picked up 10 long necks, and a junkie, and brought him home. At Bill's parents we raided their week's supply of (wild boar free) meat. His friends wanted to show me a hearty Australian barbecue.

The barbecue was electric, of course. Australians are first and foremost practical. They quickly fired up the unwashed, fatty-smelling hot plate, and whipped the grill on top. The steak was done in a flash, and was squashed between two flabby bits of white bread. We gulped the meat down as if we were standing at a draughty snack stall.

When they weren't drinking, the three chain-smoked weed, and I gave up all hope of experiencing any sort of outing on this dank day. Although I was actually already in the Bush: the garden was full of junk; old sofas and grass clippings lay around, rubbish, sodden tissues and bits of bone. When they needed to pee they stood at the fence and watered nextdoor's grass. In the corner – three or four metres away from us – two Blue Heelers yanked continually on a chain. Unlike Bill's bull terrier, they could apparently no longer get used to new people. Brad impressed on me that I must under no circumstances go near them. Hopefully his two small children, who were playing enthusiastically with the empty beer bottles, also knew that.

The house was similarly a complete tip. Leftover food was strewn over the sticky kitchen floor, and a dismantled washing machine stood in the corner. In the toilet was a thoughtfully-placed pile of porn magazines, which markedly improved both my mood and my English.

Now and then, Bill threatened a trip to a swamp, the Marshes – 'not even 200km from here. We'd camp, have a fire, a crate of beer...' he waxed lyrical about the wetland. In the face of his romanticising I was glad to be staying out drinking with his friends. By this time he was barely responsive, but it was only half past two in the afternoon. To kill time, and also to phone home, I slipped off for a walk.

When I returned an hour later, Bill had planted himself in front of the tv and had just started a dvd. He looked blissful. The fire was warm, his beer was still half full, and an excellent Hollywood action film was on: Behind Enemy Lines – about an American soldier shot down in Bosnia who was rescued by his countrymen. 'Can we start it again from the beginning?' I asked.

Ten minutes later the others also decided to watch, and asked 'Can we start it again from the beginning?'

Just as we got to the place in the film that Bill now for the third time tried to pass, the mistress of the house entered stage left. She had been shopping in the city the whole day. We stopped the film. Brad had to make a full report: how things were here, why he hadn't changed nappies, what he had done the whole day. She was not happy. Instead of answering, Brad and the others disappeared into the garden. I remained, awkwardly, sitting with her in this stranger's living room. 'Hi,' I said, hoping my expression would communicate that I wasn't here voluntarily. Eventually I found an innocent reason to get away. Beer is everything.

In Australian off licences and pubs there are signs which are supposed to inhibit excessive alcohol consumption. Included in this clearly poorly-targeted awareness campaign is the famous 'We don't serve drunks'. Luckily for Bill, he had me. But I however was warned by another sign, 'We don't sell alcohol to people buying on behalf of drunks'. But in any case, no seller gave a shit about the rules, and so Bill bought his two bottles himself.

Then we returned to the question of 'Dr', whose father Bill wanted me to meet. We stopped in the driveway. Bill opened his door with a jerk and his beer fell out. Muffled by the paper bag – it sounded like acoustic slow motion – it seemed a long time before the crack of bottle shards sounded on the concrete. We were both silent. I stared fixedly through the window. Bill breathed heavily.

'I'm very angry,' he said through clenched teeth.

'But Bill, what are bottle shops for?' I consoled him. Good idea!

At the Dr's, weed smoking was in full flow – and he really knew what he was doing. Bill said he had been big in the business for years, and in Adelaide had lived the life one imagined a dealer to have – penthouse apartment, women etc. He was then caught at the state border with a car boot full of weed. Some weeks later his photo adorned the front page of the biggest newspaper in the country. Since then he was a legend in Warren – and retrained as an electrician. But the family had had the nickname Snow even longer.

Bill quickly rang the father: 'Hi Fridge, I've got a friend here from Germany'. Wolfgang was 53 years old and hired himself out as a seasonal worker during the wheat and cotton harvest. Each Australian pronounced the surname Fritsch however he chose. However, great care was taken with the pronunciation of Wolfgang, that the 'W' should sound correctly like an 'V', and not a 'W'. However, other language niceties from his former homeland didn't make it. Although he hadn't come to Australia with his parents until he was 14, Wolfgang had virtually no German. Even with his mother he spoke English. He had been back to Germany only once, for 5 weeks – 15 years ago for his grandmother's 80th birthday. He struggled for almost half his stay to recover any German.

So we stood, the four of us, uncomfortably outside his door. It is still a puzzle to me how people in a country that prides itself on being hot can stand so long in the cold. Is that why they smoke and drink so much? Just in case Bill wasn't already seeing stars enough, coming back from pissing against the fence, he trod on a rake. It's a scene only played in comic books or American action films. The handle smacked him on the forehead with full force. And so what eight litres of beer and scores of joints hadn't managed was achieved by a well-concealed garden implement: Bill lay out cold on the wet grass.

GROOVY GRAPES

Adelaide – Ayers Rock. Unending Outback, dusty dirt roads and three-digit mileage to the next town. The Desert Patrol trip, run by Groovy Grape travel operators, was marketed with picturesque images in a Backpacker magazine. It took me three minutes to book the trip: 'Name, credit card number, you mostly sleep outdoors, please bring a sleeping bag, which hotel can we pick you up from, see you!' came succinctly over the phone.

After my time in Lake Cargelligo I spent several weeks travelling through the country, mostly to the famous tourist destinations. The first of three bus trips took me from Adelaide, the capital of the state of South Australia, across the southern half of the continent and most importantly into 'proper' Outback. This way I could see in seven days what would take weeks to do on my own: the Simpson desert, the opal city Coober Pedy, Ayers Rock, the Olgas rock formation, Kings Canyon, and Alice Springs, the city in the middle of the country.

To ensure I got up punctually, I set my watch to local time, because Australians are very exact, precise to the half hour. After the journey from Melbourne / Victoria to Adelaide /

South Australia I was still only seven hours 30 minutes ahead of Germany.

Our travel group consisted of 18 backpackers. 13 young Britons and Canadians, a young Dutch couple and two pensioners from the Black Forest, we travelled together in a small white bus with Groovy Grape written in big letters on the side. Its enormous chrome bull bar gave us a smooth ride over the 3,500km journey.

Brian, the driver and tour guide, was a down-to-earth Australian character straight out of pioneer times. He was late 30s, had lived for several years in the Outback, then exploited an opal mine in Coober Pedy, and was a real multi talent. He drove, cooked, repaired the engine and told stories. Even over the crackly loudspeakers on the bus, I could understand him astonishingly well. I had been constantly warned about the difficult Australian accent, but in fact Martin in Lake Cargelligo was the only one I had problems with. However this didn't hold true for place names. These should obviously not be easily identifiable to foreigners. Shortly after we started in Adelaide, Brian announced that we would be passing Pottagasta. I simply couldn't find it on my map. I pored over it, and asked again. Pottagasta, came again from his lips, as if it was obvious.

An hour and a half later we passed Port Augusta. Then Brian followed a 130-year-old disused railway line which ran 1,500km from the harbour city of Adelaide through the desert to Alice Springs. This legendary Ghan Line, named after the Afghan workers who built it, played an essential role in opening up the area, but was replaced years ago by a direct modern line. Overnight, the adjoining cities lost their status as busy hubs and were forgotten by the world. Abandoned diesel locomotives lay rusting on rotten tracks in the desert. Stations silted up into nothing, and at Lyndhurst – a deserted embankment without tracks – only an untouched sign showed that it was once a station. In the town of Maree, locomotives were scattered, bringing to mind an elephant graveyard, and 'for sale' had been scrawled as a joke on a bright red engine carcass. The sun shone off hole-riddled water tanks which the diesel age had long since finished off. Buffers stopped the gaze sweeping over the landscape. Points would never again decide left or right. Closed gates at level crossings seemed to wait longingly for the next train.

The ghost towns nearby – dead as after the gold rush – seemed like dilapidated stage scenery. A sign showed the crossroads between North and 12th Street, but only their foundations were visible. The only forms of life to be seen were wild camels, which grazed stoically in the Bush. Even they seemed a souvenir from a past long gone. Once the pioneers had developed the desert region and no longer needed their camels, they set their Afghan camel handlers free. And so Australia is now the only country in the world in which there are wild camels – and in such numbers that they are seen as pests and hunted.

We drove past what Brian told us was the second largest salt lake in the world, Lake Eyre. To make a more marketable superlative out of it, Australians call it 'the biggest salt lake in the southern hemisphere'. What is for sure is that it is the deepest point in the land, and the driest part of Australia – although today of course it rained. The desert character of the place is not altogether convincing, since there are over 300 springs. The National Parks Authority has made one of these into a pretty bathing spot, with a whirlpool surrounded by lush reeds.

William Creek – 168 kilometres from the next point of civilisation – had only a handful of buildings, one of which was the obligatory pub, the William Creek Hotel. Although I wouldn't have guessed it, this tiny place was a town, albeit the smallest in South Australia. More superlatives coming up later. We rolled out our mats here under the open sky, and with the wooden railway sleepers on our evening bonfire, watched another piece of the Ghan disappear.

In the morning there was dangerous two-way traffic on

the street: a light aircraft came out of the garage opposite the pub and was taking off along the road. This was how one got to work here. William Creek is encircled by Anna Creek Station, the biggest cattle farm in the world at 24,000 square kilometres. Shortly afterwards we came to the Dog Fence, at 5,600 kilometres the longest fence on the planet. Both superlatives valid even in the northern hemisphere. The Dog Fence ran across the continent from southern Queensland to western South Australia, and stopped the dingos – wild dogs which live in north Australia – from attacking the sheep herds in the southern part of the country. Dingos are the most powerful predators in Australia. I think they must have gathered on their own side of the fence, because far and wide the only thing to be seen were emus – slightly smaller than ostriches and equally unable to fly. They had their pick of all possible directions and yet always chose that which crossed our speeding bus's path. An hour later, on the open road, we had a breakdown, and the exhaust fell off. We fanned out to try and find a bit of wire to fix it back on with. Sadly the Dog Fence was by this time 60 kilometres away. Someone managed to find an actual exhaust pipe holder by the road, but it was so rusty it was no use. Brian improvised with a bit from his small spare-parts box. It would hold until Coober Pedy.

Coober Pedy is the so-called world capital of the opal gem – more than half the globe's supply comes from here. Its lunar landscape is mercilessly hot, sticky, dusty and hostile to life. The inhabitants of this rugged area therefore went underground, and established themselves in the former mines, which have a constant comfortable temperature of 24 degrees. The people play out almost their entire social life – with the exception of swimming in the outdoor pool – either underground or by night, for example golf by flood lights. Outside I saw only underground entrances, streets, car parks and some few buildings. If somebody's flat gets too small, he simply has an excavation machine come, and in next to no time a new room is cheaply added on. Flats with 10 or 20 rooms are therefore standard.

Our group also searched for opals on an abandoned plot, inspired by Brian's incredible stories of travellers going home stinking rich from the area. But an hour digging in the scree ended without success, and in the absence of treasure, we fell back on the Bedrock Hotel as planned for the night. Underground as the other buildings, it rather brought to mind a missile bunker. Left and right off a long neon-lit corridor were small bays each with two bunk beds hammered into the mine tunnels.

Brian's call at 4.30am woke us all, including those in other travel groups. We had 730km to travel today, from Coober Pedy to Yulara, where Ayers Rock lies. On the morning roads lay lots of dead kangaroos, run over and now descended on by birds. Suddenly on the open road Brian came screeching to a halt, ran 100m back and lunged over the verge. Proudly he presented us with a Thorny Devil, a type of mini lizard studded with 'thorns'. It was cute. They are totally harmless, and it even let us stroke it. We later learned that every travel group had such an experience. But you surely couldn't arrange such a stunt in the Outback? 10 minutes later the next unscheduled event: steam came hissing out of the air con. We tripped off the bus and sought cover in the Bush. Luckily it turned out to be only compressed air, but for the next few days we had no air conditioning and had to make do with only open windows and the breeze of motion.

And then finally we arrived at Ayers Rock, named Uluru by the native Anangu people. It was suddenly in front of us, dominating the horizon. Powerful, red, towering over everything. The sunset glowed off its skin. Everyone is drawn to this enormous 'stone'. It's not in fact a monolith, but a part of a larger, underground layer of rock. Like an iceberg, it stretches down two and a half kilometres, but protrudes only 348 metres. Here too I experienced the world differently: normally with a sunset you look at the sun, but here, the rock drew all eyes magnetically to itself. Its red shadows changed by the minute, until the mountain was only visible as a dark backdrop.

And then in the morning the opposite: the rock lay squat like a tree stump, dark and lifeless in the landscape, until the first warm rays of sunshine tickled it awake. Its wonderful red colour returned. I didn't want to leave, I wanted to stay there forever and hang onto that rosy reflected sunlight. Or at least I would were it not for the group of 100 other tourists, who, three minutes after draining the cava from their plastic glasses, hopped back into their buses and reversed noisily in convoy. So much for the atmosphere. Brian waited, but only another five minutes – we still had much to do that morning.

So we didn't climb onto the Uluru until much later, in the heat of midday, although the best conditions are early morning. I know that it's not only unwise from a climbing point of view, but that it is also totally politically incorrect. The Anangu don't want climbers, not least because they grieve when something happens to a tourist.

Our biggest test came right at the beginning. The way up was steep. Very steep. The sun beat down mercilessly. Luckily I could haul myself up using a chain which hung from small posts anchored in the ground. But we still had to stop every minute in order to sit down and rest. Every minute. My heart raced, my pulse thundered. We pulled ourselves together again, and then the sun immediately burnt us back again and dried out our bodies even further. Ten metres later another break. Everyone hung onto the chain. How did the tourist hordes go up and down in one piece every single day? Aha, they made the climb early. It was steep, hot, and in some places one false step would be enough – directly next to the chain was the edge of the precipice.

50 metres to go, and then the first and most difficult leg was done. After that it was flat until the summit itself.

So the people passing us on their way down encouraged us. They all looked totally relaxed. But we still had 50 metres of pounding hearts to go until a quarter of the way was done. Metre by metre we pulled ourselves up, until we reached a small platform. The worst was behind us.

Ahead was a large plateau. Like on a marathon route, the stretch was painted in colour, but I can't describe it as a racing line. It was a stony obstacle course through huge channels and over walls two metres high.

Finally! We had made it. Exhausted and breathing hard we fell by the summit stone and drank up all our remaining water before we could concentrate on the view. The stark colour contrasts were intoxicating. After months of rain, trees, bushes and grass were a deep green, the sand glowed red, the sky was blue and decorated with white, low-hanging cloud. On the horizon lay the equally beautiful but less well-known Olga mountains.

We had done it! We felt as if we had scaled half of Everest, although in fact we were only at 348m altitude. A British man rang home from the summit. Some of us were yet to recover the power of speech.

A HOT ENDING

Darwin, Kakadu National Park. Their names were Jessica, Jennifer and Jane, and together called themselves Triple J, like the famous Australian radio station. These three pensioners permanently cracked jokes, laughed, and flirted with Richard, the 55-year old driver who in profile looked like a famous German politician. We were spending three days travelling through the Kakadu National Park to the northern edge of Australia in a cross country bus, mostly on proper roads but sometimes through streams. This tour didn't have the usual backpacker mix. Aside from the three merry widows from Sydney, other participants looking for a neatly-packaged adventure were:

- A Japanese lady, who after four months of English lessons still couldn't make herself understood.
- A 50-year-old Welshman, who only had two teeth in his upper jaw, and spoke with such an accent as to make me believe that English was his second, seldom-used language. I shared a room with him, and he made noises on breathing out when asleep the like of which I had never heard before. The amiable, unworldly old chap wore ear plugs and an eye mask at night, alt-

hough I was the one who needed them.
- An Indonesian couple of Chinese origin, who owned a factory in Jakarta. He had studied in England, she in the US. They spoke the best English of everyone.

To initiate us into Crocodile Dundee country right from the beginning, and to stretch out the suspense, the tour began spectacularly with a boat trip on the Mary River. Crocodiles could be tempted with meat on a hook. Scarcely had the guide hung the rod with the lump of meat over the railing, when three of the beasts slid soundlessly past for their daily rations. Picture perfect, they leapt up a metre and a half to take the prey, and withdrew again, munching. Reptiles didn't go hungry that morning. Then we were on to the next animal attraction – seven-metre tall termite mounds. They stood in the landscape like brown cathedrals, each one home to over a million termites. The queen can live to the age of 50, and lays 20,000 eggs a day.

The heat was relentless, and we wanted only one thing: SWIMMING. In a swimming pool, of course, not a billabong – a water hole – since crocodiles weren't so far away. We halted the Bush programme for the day and headed early afternoon to our campsite and its pool.

That evening round the campfire we experienced the obligatory Aborigine didgeridoo performance. Virtually naked and traditionally painted, a local man led us with the strange, deep, spherically vibrating drone of his instrument into the emotional world of his people. We weren't the only listeners. Dark silhouettes clustered round us as a second row: wallabies. These mini kangaroos weren't disturbed by either us or the music. Or perhaps the didgeridoo player enticed them, as an Australian Pied Piper?

The kangaroos stayed until morning, trimming the grass. They more than made up for the long kangaroo-free time we'd had so far. There were over 100 animals, and as though a considerate part of the campsite service, they let themselves be stroked and didn't jump away. To get to the showers, we had to do a slalom course.

Top of today's programme was rock paintings and an idyllic stone landscape at Nourlangie Rock. Officially. But it was again unbearably hot and muggy, and after a two-hour tour of the ancient yet unmistakable drawings of penises, once again all we wanted to do was swim. We didn't care where, just as long as it was cool. There was no pool nearby, and so our driver-leader-cook took us this time into the wild, allegedly far from crocodiles or aggressive water buffalo. It took until sundown for us to feel active again, when we climbed to a small plateau to watch the day fade away with a cup of red wine. The last rays of the sun illuminated faraway rocks, Bushland and the distant, drying billabongs which emerge during the rainy season.

The third day was no cooler, and so there was only one thing on the agenda: a waterfall, which thanks to the recent rainy season was in full flow. Amongst the cascades, the current had formed convenient sitting places and holes to plunge into. The waters fizzed through so cleverly that a natural whirlpool had formed outside. And while the fresh mountain water streamed over my shoulders, I looked from the edge of the top step back into the shimmering valley.

WORLDVISION SONG CONTEST

The background: I was spending three days on Fraser Island in Queensland with 30 backpackers from 15 different countries. Fraser Island is the biggest sand island in the world – 100km long, 25km wide, covered with forest and blessed with 80 clear lakes. Apart from some crags, the subsoil of the island consists entirely of sand. To travel around, we were in a desert-designed, four-wheel-drive bus. The second day of our trip led us along the coast to the remote North, to Indian Head, a cape where we could see whales, dolphins, turtles and sharks. The wide sandy beach that leads there is officially a road and a busy one at that.

   2.30pm: We saw all the promised sea creatures during a ten-minute lunchbreak at Indian Head. Ronald, our bus driver, then started talking already about leaving – appointments were pressing. He had to have 16 of our troop at the harbour at the other end of the island by 5pm. They had to catch the evening bus on the mainland to get to their pre-booked sailing trip through the Whitsunday Islands, 700km north.
   2.31pm: Ronald turned on the sand, in the direction of the sea, where the waves peter out and trickle away into

the sand. He floored the accelerator... and the truck stayed exactly where it was. The wheels turned, and although we were by now clearly stuck, Ronald rammed the accelerator to the floor another two times. Nothing moved. 'Get out!' he cried.

The bottom step met the wet sand, and we sank ankle deep in sludge. The Danish couple took their rucksack with them. We laughed at such pessimism, since it was still nearly an hour and a half until the tide would reach us. By then we would be long since on our way.

On all four sides, the wheels were sunk up to the axles. Ronald began to dig, but the holes filled immediately with water. 40 hands could help him, but there was only one shovel. We must have entered the Bermuda triangle of the island. Around us were several other stranded four-by-fours, which were being swiftly pulled out by jeeps. Ronald wondered whether that would work for our bus. A single car would clearly not be powerful enough, but surely two together could get us out of this jam...

2.55pm: Two Toyota Landcruisers took up position one behind the other at the back of the bus. Ronald gave the starter's signal and put the bus into reverse. He whooped and hollered, the wheels turned in the water. But the only thing that moved was the tow cable, which broke and smashed one of the Toyota's headlights.

2.59pm: Ronald handed over the firm's details for the insurance for the headlight damage, and reeled in the cable. The sea drove its waves nearer the bus. Our helpers drove their cars out of the danger zone.

3.05pm: Shouldn't I perhaps get my camera out of the bus and just take a couple of pictures?

3.10pm: Popular tourist destination Indian Head has one more attraction. The first group of tourists gathered and took pictures. Deep sea fishermen and men on booze cruises made themselves comfortable and commentated sagely on the rescue attempt.

3.12pm: The first unrest spread amongst those who urgently had to catch the 5pm ferry. Ronald said he didn't think they would get it. They would have to cross on the 8pm boat. But it was already clear: they wouldn't make the connection and would all miss their sailing trip the next morning through one of Australia's top travel destinations. For the Dutch the dream trip was probably lost forever: they were flying home in five days and weren't sure they would ever come back to Australia in their lives.

3.18pm: I got my camera from the bus.

3.24pm: A tourist bus broke rank with the sightseeing crowd to rescue us.

3.30pm: Second attempt. A board was laid under the left front wheel. All men present must get ready to push.

3.31pm: The water smelt brackish. We were wading deep in sludge. Then both vehicles revved their engines.

3.32pm: Nothing moved. The other bus pulled back.

3.33pm: I wondered whether I shouldn't also get my rucksack?

The beach filled up. Bus parties prolonged their trip, families posed for pictures, telling jokes. The fact that this morning, 40km south of here, we had been gazing at the 70-year old wreck of the former luxury steamboat Maheno suddenly seemed an uncomfortable parallel. We suggested that our stranded bus be incorporated into the next tour programme. If photos were needed for the advertising brochure – no problem there.

3.40pm: I got my rucksack out of the bus.

3.42pm: Woo, the Korean man, gave me his address so that I could send him photos. His camera was still inside the bus.

4.01pm: The sea reached the bus and swirled underneath. Everyone who hadn't yet removed their belongings, hurried to do so.

4.05pm: Woo's address was no longer necessary. He was photographing everything himself.

4.10pm: Ronald announced that he had requested a

new vehicle. He didn't tell us that it would take at least three hours to reach us.

4.12pm: People began to run out of film. I wondered how much I could sell my last films for?

4.13pm: Woo deleted from his new digital camera previous sights now deemed unimportant.

4.16pm: Tony, the Englishman, saved one frame 'for the final shot'.

4.20pm: A representative from the group of American teenagers started complaining that we were stuck. She didn't want to miss the expensive sailing trip and would like to leave straightaway. She asked angrily about compensation and customer service, and withdrew crossly. I didn't tell her that the three other Americans, who weren't part of her group of friends, were lawyers.

4.23pm: Ian, an Australian, suggested that the bus be given over as a tourist attraction for future outings. We told him we'd already had that idea at 3.33pm.

4.30pm: Shoptalk with the boozed-up locals told us the bus was already considered lost. It had apparently often happened with cars, but never before with such a big vehicle. They found the title 'Ranger Guided Tour' on the side of the bus most amusing.

4.35pm: The Danes suggested to Ronald that he get the food and water box out of the hold.

4.37pm: There were muesli bars, oranges, and cold water.

5pm: The tide reached the passenger cabin.

5.01pm: Katrin, a social-education student from Austria, asked me whether the bus wouldn't be damaged if it 'got wet inside'.

5.04pm: An American woman was stung by an unknown insect in the dunes, and in floods of tears showed Ronald her swollen arm.

5.10pm: Suddenly a tow truck appeared. The chances of making the 8 o'clock ferry rose. But our bus was twice as long, probably three times as heavy, and the sea had meanwhile advanced so far up the beach, that the lorry could only pull from a 50m distance and a 45 degree angle. Ronald dived down to the bumper to fasten the chain to the bus.

5.11pm: The sun sank lower – great light for photos.

5.15pm: The tow truck started its winch and the cable tautened. Respectfully we sought cover behind the cars. We were afraid the cable might break. We all agreed: 'If the breakdown truck had come an hour and a half ago... but now?'

5.21pm: The tow truck gave up and drove off to safety.

5.24pm: A forceful wave set our bus rocking. I ate my muesli bar.

5.27pm: Tony was waiting until the bus actually sank into the sea for his last photo.

5.30pm: One of the Dutch women wrote down the names of the people who had wanted to be away half an hour ago. Was she preparing a class lawsuit?

5.32pm: Woo wanted to take a souvenir picture of him and me in front of the bus. He was happy with the third take.

5.35pm: Some tourists asked me whether this was the second attraction on the coast after the Maheno Wreck. We'd had that idea already at 3.33pm.

5.40pm: A National Parks Ranger asked all onlookers to get back away from the incoming water.

5.42pm: The tow truck drove off.

5.43pm: A bulldozer moved in. We tried to place bets, but no one would bet on rescue. Everyone was agreed: 'If the bulldozer had come 90 minutes ago... but now?'

5.44pm: It was getting a bit dark for good photos.

5.45pm: 'Ronald, how much does a bus like that cost?' Answer, '300,000 dollars.' (180,000 euros).

5.50pm: The bulldozer tried to pull the bus out, at an angle of 40 degrees.

5.52pm: Nothing moved.

5.55pm: Tony was still waiting for his final picture.

5.56pm: The replacement bus still wasn't there. I was slowly getting cold, since I had on only a t-shirt and shorts. Nevertheless, I realised that I had got sunburnt in the last few hours.

6.03pm: It was dark. The other tourists had departed for their resorts. We were alone with the bulldozer and the rangers. Like a weeble, the bus returned to the same position after every wave.

6.10pm: The 8 o'clock ferry was no longer a possibility.

6.11pm: Ronald told us the replacement bus was on its way. We could wait for it in a hostel behind the dunes. We marvelled that there was a piece of civilisation in this remote place. The time of the last ferry was apparently 11pm.

6.20pm: The hostel owners served coffee, tea and cake. We were in luck: normally they were booked up, but we had caught them on the changeover day between departure and arrivals.

6.25pm: There was beer and cola. Anyone who wanted could take himself off to bed.

6.30pm: The beer ran out.

6.32pm: New supplies of beer arrived.

6.35pm: Even more beer arrived.

6.37pm: Also on offer: Cola-Whisky.

6.40pm: We wondered at an original, home-made iron contraption on the table.

6.42pm: The hostel owner showed us how a beer-can press worked. It was the hit of the evening. Everyone wanted to crush their own can. That cranked up the beer consumption. It was an ongoing cycle.

6.45pm: Someone handed out cards and a scrabble board.

6.50pm: Our refuge was only reachable over the beach. We learnt from the radio that the replacement bus couldn't get through because of the tide.

6.52pm: Our host put two bottles of rum on every table. We didn't need a replacement bus anymore.

6.54pm: Ronald was not impressed with the rum idea and handed the bottles back. The can crusher was back to full throttle.

7.05pm: While Peder, the Swede, was having a pee in the Bush, a snake slithered between his legs.

7.30pm: The bus wouldn't be there before 10.30. The hostel warden grilled some tailor fish he had caught himself. We would be happy to extend our stay.

7.34pm: I was appointed chief can crusher.

7.36pm: I introduced a Swedish girl to an Australian woman – they both had Philippino parents.

7.40pm: The Korean man realised that one of the American women was originally from Korea. But they couldn't communicate – he had hardly any English, and she spoke no Korean.

7.47pm: The Ranger distributed blankets.

7.55pm: The faces of the Dutch and American women who were missing their sailing trip grew ever longer.

8.10pm: The tailor fish was ready.

8.30pm: A couple of the group insisted on crushing their own cans.

8.50pm: After some group dynamics games, we explained to the Americans about the Eurovision Song Contest. They loved it, and we started a sort of Worldvision Song Contest.

9.07pm: Tony suggested that each person sang their national anthem. America started. But everyone knew that one.

'Is the English anthem the same as the British one?' asked someone. 'Is it God save the Queen?'

If there is one day a King, will the text change?

Germany has two anthems, so as a bonus we also did the GDR's version. We still only got one set of points – a seven.

Korea: ten points. Corée: dix points. Now everyone was listening. The first big round of applause.

'Our anthem is all about hope,' announced the Israeli couple. We nodded encouragingly.

The Dutch hymn had 15 verses. They did only a short version though. In contrast to Germany they only sang the first verse.

'How many points can I give Austria?' I asked myself.

Marga, a Finnish lady, fussed about. 'You've had ten minutes to practise!' said Host Tony, strictly.

A huge military helicopter hovered above us. Headlights lit up the surroundings.

'It's the Marines come to rescue the Americans!' we joked.

'Who hasn't sung yet?' Tony wanted to know.

The Australians sang their unofficial anthem, Waltzing Matilda.

'Who or what *is* Matilda?' everybody wondered.

A type of mattress.

Joking aside, the army helicopter actually did rescue an American – the woman who had been stung by an insect in the dunes. The ranger had called for it because her arm was so swollen. Sadly, they would only take the patient, otherwise the Dutch couple could have made their connecting bus.

Sweden had until now successfully wriggled out of it, but Tony was merciless. Finland was still running through the words, last call for Denmark.

Then sang the blonde Valkyrie: 'Oi maamme, Suomi, synnyinmaa!' As with all the non-English lyrics, no one had any idea if the words were correct, but it sounded Finnish, and her professional performance was like that of the plumpest opera singer. Her rehearsal had paid off: neuf points.

Could Sweden knock Korea off the top spot? 'Du gamla, Du fria, Du fjällhöga nord' reached at least third place.

11.30pm: It was actually 11.30pm. We had forgotten everything around us. The replacement bus had arrived. We must go.

The winner is... Korea.

Woo took a deep bow.

LIST OF TRANSPORTATION

1. Aeroplane – Cessna 232

2. Private car / flatbed truck

3. Tour bus / lorry – Groovy Grape among others

4. Train – Ghan

5. Courtesy Bus

6. Army helicopter

LIST OF SUPERLATIVES

1. Lake Eyre – The lowest point and – when full – the largest lake in Australia
2. William Creek – The smallest town in the state of South Australia
3. Anna Creek Station – The biggest cattle farm in the world
4. Dog Fence – The longest fence in the world
5. Coober Pedy – 'World Capital of Opals'
6. Fraser Island – Biggest sand island in the world

ALEX TANNEN

Alex Tannen (a pseudonym) is in his 40s and is a native Berliner.

Since his student days (Political Sciences and MBA), he has travelled extensively, often alone and mostly in Arab and African countries. His trips have taken him from the Gaza Strip, via Libya and Timbuktu, to Germany's lake-district Mecklenburg, where he realised as he paddled in the idyll that he could do without a passport.

He has published four travel books in German. 'Victoria Bitter - Stories from an Australian Winter', about an internship in an Australian construction company in 2003, is his first book translated into English.